# Revive and Thrive: The Art of Business Turnaround

## Executive Summary: At a Glance

**Introduction**
**Transformative Turnaround: Unleashing the Power of Business Resilience**

Welcome to "Transformative Turnaround: Unleashing the Power of Business Resilience," a captivating journey into the heart of revitalizing organizations and embracing the dynamic world of business. In the realm of ever-evolving markets, disruptive technologies, and unforeseen challenges, the art of business turnaround is a beacon of hope and transformation.

In this transformative book, we explored the essential elements that paved the path to success amidst uncertainty. From the visionary leadership that ignites the spark of change to crafting the rescue plan that breathes life back into struggling enterprises, we delve into the strategies that defy the odds and redefine success.

The essence of collaboration and synergy comes alive as we witness the tremendous power of teams working in unison, overcoming obstacles and achieving the extraordinary. We discover how continuous improvement becomes the heartbeat of organizations, nurturing a culture of adaptability that thrives in the face of change.

As we journey through the pages, real-life examples of iconic companies such as Microsoft, Apple, and Tesla will inspire and illuminate. These beacons of innovation have forged their destinies through relentless determination and the courage to embrace the unknown.
From fostering strategic partnerships and driving social responsibility to preparing for the future through innovation and emerging technologies, each chapter reveals the secrets to sustainability and long-term growth. We witness the impact of a growth mindset, where curiosity, learning, and progress become catalysts for greatness.

Through the lens of the transformative journey, we see the transformative potential within each reader. Whether you are a visionary leader seeking to steer your organization towards triumph or an aspiring entrepreneur with a dream to revolutionize industries, this book will equip you with the tools to thrive in the face of uncertainty.

So, join us on this transformative odyssey as we navigate the twists and turns of business turnaround. Together, we shall unlock the power of resilience and adaptability, paving the way to an inspiring future where innovation, compassion, and sustainable growth reign supreme.
Are you ready to embrace the art of business turnaround? Then let us embark on this transformative journey together and unlock the boundless potential that lies within you. The dynamic world of business awaits your triumphant arrival - let's seize the opportunities and build a future of limitless possibilities.

# Chapter One
## Introduction and Planning

Welcome to "Revive and Thrive: The Art of Business Turnaround!" This chapter focuses on recognizing early warning signs that signal when your business is facing crisis. Rapid identification of such indicators is vital in taking proactive measures and steering away from potential disasters. Let's look at key signs of trouble as well as understand industry-specific challenges to bolster your organization against stormy waters.

**Early Identification of Business Crises:** It can be crucial for business survival to detect early warning signs of crises to avert major setbacks. So, paying close attention to your performance and gathering pertinent data is key to spotting any warning signals that might apply to your situation. Ask yourself these questions when searching for warning signals:

1. Have your sales figures experienced significant fluctuations over the last quarter or two? Have they compared favorably with

historical data, and have any patterns been noticed?

2. Have you seen an increase in customer complaints or a sudden decrease in satisfaction scores, and taken steps to address these concerns and retain customer loyalty? If so, what steps have been taken?

3. Are your operational costs increasing rapidly and financial obligations becoming difficult to fulfill? Have you analyzed key cost drivers and explored cost-cutting measures? If that is the case for your organization, and costs have spiked beyond expectations, have you investigated and identified ways of cutting expenses?

4. Have there been any changes in market demand, technological innovations or consumer behaviour affecting your industry that impact how you conduct business? How have you adjusted your strategies accordingly?

**Industry-Specific Challenges:** Each industry presents unique difficulties, and being aware of these problems can bolster your resilience during difficult times. Consider asking the following questions about your industry to gain an understanding of its dynamics:

1. What are the key challenges businesses in your industry are currently facing and how have these changed over time? Have there been any successful turnaround cases within your sector?
2. How does your business compare with competitors in terms of market share and customer loyalty? What distinguishes it, and how can it take advantage of its strengths during a turnaround process?

3. Have any regulatory or industry trends emerged that could impose on your industry soon, and how are you planning to adapt proactively to them?

4. How will your business be affected by any impending economic shifts or geopolitical events? Have you developed contingency plans to mitigate potential risks?

By recognizing early warning signs and understanding industry-specific challenges, you'll be better equipped to steer your business through crisis and chart a course towards recovery and growth. In the following chapter, we'll cover how to conduct an extensive assessment to uncover the root causes of its decline and create effective turnaround strategies - get ready to unleash its power!

**The Art of Business Turnaround:** Adopting Change during Times of Crisis

Faced with economic turmoil and obstacles to their growth, businesses often find themselves on the verge of collapse. Navigating this challenging road from decline to revival requires courage; but for those willing to accept this task and face up to its challenges head-on, it offers great potential for transformation and growth. In this chapter, we explore the art of business turnaround as well as the essential steps required to weather any crisis towards a brighter future.

**Understanding the Need for Turnaround:** A business turnaround occurs when a company facing financial distress, declining performance or operational inefficiency implements a strategic plan to change their fortunes. A turnaround may arise for various reasons such as market disruptions, increased competition, leadership issues or macroeconomic shocks.

One real-life example of a successful business turnaround can be seen through Harley-Davidson. Beginning in the early 1980s, this iconic American motorcycle manufacturer experienced declining sales, financial losses and fierce competition from Japanese motorcycle makers. Under CEO Vaughn Beals's guidance, however, Harley-Davidson implemented an effective turnaround plan focused on improving product quality, strengthening dealer relationships and increasing customer loyalty - within five years Harley's fortunes had reversed and it regained its position as an industry powerhouse (source: Harley-Davidson Annual Report, various years).

**At the Heart of Successful Business Turnaround - Vision and Leadership:** A key element of any successful business turnaround lies at its core - visionary leaders understand the challenges confronted by an organization, set an exciting direction for its future, inspire their teams to embrace change and unite behind a common purpose.

Steve Jobs at Apple Inc. is an impressive example of visionary leadership during a turnaround scenario. In the late '90s, Apple faced declining market share and financial losses; when Steve returned as CEO he immediately initiated several bold moves - such as launching innovative products like the iMac and then later iPod, iPhone, and iPad. Through his unwavering dedication and customer-first focus Jobs transformed Apple into one of the world's most valuable technology firms (source: "The Second Coming of Steve Jobs by Alan Deutschman). Conduct a Comprehensive Business Assessment In order to effectively begin their turnaround journey, businesses must first conduct an in-depth assessment of their current state. This may involve reviewing financial statements, operational processes and key performance indicators as well as key performance indicators in order to identify areas of concern and plan an approach.

Best Buy Co. Inc. is an excellent example of an assessment leading to a successful business turnaround. In early 2010, this consumer electronics retailer faced declining sales, becoming a victim of "Amazon effect." As Hubert Joly led, Best Buy's management team undertook an intensive business assessment in order to pinpoint inefficiencies and prioritize strategic initiatives, cost-cutting measures were implemented along with store renovations and increased customer experience focus; ultimately resulting in its stock price skyrocketing and customer satisfaction reaching new heights (source: "The Turnaround of Best Buy," by Vijay Govindarajan and Anup Srivastava of Harvard Business School case study).

Once an assessment is complete, the next critical step in the turnaround process is identifying the root causes of business decline. These could range from poor financial management and ineffective marketing strategies, operational bottlenecks or external market forces as potential sources.
At IBM (International Business Machines Corporation), root cause identification during business turnaround was demonstrated through CEO Louis V. Gerstner Jr's analysis. When IBM faced serious challenges during the early 1990s - including declining profits and market share - Louis recognized its limited potential due to focusing on hardware products alone as its

only focus (source: Louis V. Gerstner Jr). Through identifying this fundamental flaw, IBM changed direction by moving away from hardware products towards software products and services, ultimately leading to long-term growth (source: Louis V. Gerstner Jr).

**Establishing a Diagnosis Report:** The results of business assessments and the identification of root causes result in the creation of a comprehensive diagnosis report, serving as the backbone for creating a turnaround plan by outlining the current state, challenges faced, potential ramifications if left unaddressed, etc.

One such diagnosis report that led to a successful business turnaround can be seen at McDonald's Corporation in the early 2000s. At that time, this fast-food giant saw sales decrease and customers losing trust in its brand image. McDonald's conducted an in-depth diagnosis, which identified menu complexity, slow service and increased competition as its chief challenges. Armed with this insight, McDonald's developed and implemented a strategic plan which included menu simplification, improved operational efficiencies, and an emphasis on customer experience. As a result, their stock price witnessed a dramatic increase and customer satisfaction rebounded (source: Niraj Dawar's "McDonald's Turnaround", Harvard Business Review).

Conclusion Successful business turnaround requires an ideal combination of visionary leadership, data-driven analysis, and the courage to embrace change. Real-life examples like Harley-Davidson, Apple, Best Buy, IBM and McDonald's demonstrate this truth with successful turnarounds like Harley-Davidson, Apple, Best Buy IBM and McDonald's all showing this potential success story. In the next chapter, we will delve deeper into strategies for crafting rescue plans that target identified challenges while setting up for recovery - get ready for an incredible journey towards brighter days!

# Chapter 2
## Assessing Damage: Diagnosing the Root Causes of Business Decline

This chapter introduces the critical process of evaluating damage and diagnosing root causes of business decline. Understanding these core challenges is vital in creating effective turnaround strategies to address them successfully. Let's explore various methodologies and tools which will provide greater insights into your company's current state and pave the way towards a successful recovery.

**Conduct a Comprehensive Business Assessment:** To kick-off the diagnostic process, it is crucial to conduct an extensive business assessment. Review financial statements, operational processes and performance metrics closely in order to identify any areas of concern. Tools like SWOT analysis (Strengths, Weaknesses, Opportunities and Threats) may be utilized for internal strengths and weaknesses analysis along with external opportunities and threats evaluation. Obtain feedback from employees and key stakeholders so as to gain an encompassing view of your organization's issues.

1. How will you collect data for the business assessment, and which key performance indicators will you focus on?
2. Have you identified any internal strengths that can be leveraged during a turnaround process and specific weaknesses that need to be addressed?
3. Which external opportunities can be taken advantage of, and how will you mitigate potential threats to business recovery?
4. Have key stakeholders such as employees and customers been included in the assessment process so as to gain valuable insights from diverse viewpoints?

**After Collecting Relevant Data Identify the Root Causes:** It is critical that once you have collected relevant data, you identify and address the fundamental causes for your business's decline. These might include poor financial management, ineffective marketing strategies, operational inefficiencies or external market forces affecting performance. Be prepared to dig deep and address these fundamental issues affecting the performance of your organization.

1. From your assessment, what are the primary root causes contributing to the business's decline?
2. Based on this knowledge, how will you prioritize these root causes to focus on only the most vital issues during the turnaround process?
3. Have you identified any systemic issues that may be impacting multiple aspects of the business's operations? 4. Are there external factors influencing your decline and how can you adapt to them?

**Create a Diagnosis Report:** Once your findings are compiled, compile them into a detailed diagnosis report that clearly and objectively details its current state, root causes identified, potential implications if unaddressed and the best turnaround strategies to take. Your diagnosis report can serve as an excellent source for informing targeted turnaround strategies.

1. What structure will you employ when writing the diagnosis report so as to present

assessment findings and root cause analysis effectively?

2. Which key data points and visualizations will you incorporate into the report in support of your analysis and conclusions?

3. How will you communicate the diagnosis report to key stakeholders, and secure their support for the proposed turnaround strategies?

4. Is the diagnosis report an evolving living document that will be regularly referenced during the turnaround process?

By performing an in-depth assessment and diagnosing its root causes, you will create an ideal environment for crafting effective turnaround strategies. Over the coming chapters, we will cover how to create a tailored rescue plan to address identified challenges while setting your business on its path toward revival and long-term success. Get ready for an exciting transformation journey!

# Chapter 3
## Crafting The Rescue Plan

**Crafting the Rescue Plan:** Strategies for Business Turnaround Introduction In the previous chapter, we explored the significance of understanding why business turnaround is necessary and how visionary leadership can lead the transformation journey. Now, let us move into crafting our rescue plan; in this section, we explore strategies and key elements necessary to create an effective turnaround plan that addresses challenges identified with the recovery and growth of any given company.

**Assess Key Challenges and Prioritize Initiatives:** The first step in creating a rescue plan is identifying key challenges facing your business and prioritizing initiatives with the greatest impact for recovery. This means identifying the root causes behind its decline as well as crafting specific strategies to tackle them.

Ford Motor Company provided an outstanding example of effective turnaround planning during the Great

Recession of 2008-2009. As sales began to fall and losses mounted, its management team led by CEO Alan Mulally conducted a comprehensive assessment of the company's challenges; their focus included debt reduction, quality enhancement and creating fuel efficient vehicles.

Ford emerged stronger and more resilient due to these strategic initiatives, becoming the only major American automaker not to declare bankruptcy during the economic crisis (source: "American Icon: Alan Mulally and the Fight to Save Ford Motor Company," by Bryce G. Hoffman).

**Establish Clear Goals and Objectives:** To maximize turnaround efforts effectively, it is critical to establish specific and measurable goals and objectives that align with the vision of the business and are communicated across all levels of an organization to ensure everyone is working towards one common destination.

Starbucks Corporation provided an outstanding example of setting clear goals during a turnaround in the early 2000s. After experiencing declining sales and increased competition, Howard Schultz, as founder and CEO, returned to lead his company and set ambitious goals that would reinvigorate growth while improving the Starbucks experience - such as expanding store footprint, bolstering customer loyalty, and revamping store layouts. By following through with their turnaround plan with precision, the goals were accomplished successfully, leading them back onto the global coffee scene (source: "Onward: How Starbucks Fought for its Life without Losing Its Soul", by Howard Schultz).

**Financial Restructuring and Cost Optimization:** When dealing with financial distress, restructuring is often an integral component of the rescue plan. This involves analyzing a business's capital structure, renegotiating debts, and optimizing costs to improve cash flow and enhance financial stability.

General Motors (GM), for instance, demonstrated successful financial restructuring during the 2008-2009 economic crisis. Facing serious financial difficulties and filing for bankruptcy protection, GM underwent an intensive financial restructuring plan as part of its rescue plan, including debt reduction and plant closure/streamlining initiatives.

GM emerged from bankruptcy restructured as a leaner and more efficient company that was prepared for long-term growth (source: "American Turnaround: Reinventing AT&T and GM to Do Business in the USA", by Edward Whitacre Jr).

**Operational Efficiency and Process Improvement:** Enhancing operational efficiency is a cornerstone of a rescue plan, helping businesses optimize resources and boost productivity. Process improvement initiatives aim to eliminate inefficiencies from operations while simultaneously increasing effectiveness overall.

Delta Air Lines stands as an exemplary case of operational efficiency and process improvement during a turnaround scenario. At the start of 2000s, airlines faced numerous difficulties, such as increased competition and rising fuel costs. Led by CEO Richard Anderson, Delta implemented several changes that included fleet optimization, route rationalization, and enhanced maintenance practices - all within just seven years!

These initiatives resulted in cost reduction and enhanced operational performance, contributing to Delta's turnaround and sustained profitability (source: Robert E. Spekman and Robert F. Bruner's book entitled "Delta Air Lines (A): The Low-Cost Carrier Threat", Darden Business Publishing).

**Innovation Plays an Essential Part in Turnaround Success:** New and innovative products or services can play a crucial role in helping a business turn its fortunes around. Businesses can reinvigorate customer engagement while strengthening competitive edges within their market by reinvigorating customer interest and increasing competitive advantages in the marketplace.

LEGO Group provides an outstanding example of product innovation as a catalyst for turnaround. In the early 2000s, when faced with declining consumer preferences and competition from digital entertainment services like Star Wars and Harry Potter franchises, it introduced new lines of products focused on creative building experiences and collaboration with popular franchises like these - this innovative approach not only revitalized LEGO's brand but also led to significant increases in sales and profitability (source: "Brick by Brick: How LEGO Rewrote the Rules of Innovation and Conquered the Global Toy Industry" by David Robertson & Bill Breen).

**Engaging Employees and Stakeholders:** Successful turnaround plan implementation hinges upon engaging employees and stakeholders effectively. Open, honest communication among all parties involved must take place for all to work toward one common goal - recovery.

Royal Dutch Shell in the early 2000s offers an illuminating example of employee and stakeholder engagement during a turnaround: declining profitability and high-profile accidents were major concerns, so CEO Jeroen van der Veer initiated an open, transparent culture where employees discussed challenges facing the company as well as potential solutions; this engagement fostered employee ownership and commitment, leading to improved safety records and operational efficiencies (source: "Shell Shocked: How Shell Built a Sustainable Business through Employee Engagement," by Malcolm S. McDonald and Joe Peppard).

## Conclusion

Establishing an in-depth rescue plan is the cornerstone of a successful business turnaround. This chapter's strategies, such as assessing key challenges and setting clear goals; financial restructuring; optimizing costs; improving operations; innovating products and engaging stakeholders have proven highly successful in real-life turnaround situations. Businesses can weather any crisis more easily by developing an effective rescue plan and devising an actionable rescue strategy. We will explore the vital role leadership has in inspiring change and driving recovery within an organization - so get ready to lead with vision and purpose on the road back!

# Chapter 4
## Crafting Rescue Plans: Formulating Effective Turnaround Strategies

Now that you understand the causes of your business's decline, it's time to develop a comprehensive rescue plan. In this chapter, we will explore the art of crafting effective turnaround strategies to address identified challenges and propel recovery. A plan designed specifically for your needs can ensure sustainable growth as you navigate the crisis.

**Understanding Turnaround Strategies:** Before diving deeper, let's review various turnaround strategies frequently used to revitalize struggling businesses. These might include cost reduction measures, product/service diversification, market expansion, or restructuring altogether. Carefully consider which approaches best fit your unique situation as identified by the diagnosis report and the root causes uncovered during diagnosis.

1. Which turnaround strategies address your business's current challenges while aligning with long-term goals?
2. How will you prioritize and sequence these strategies to ensure an integrated and effective approach?
3. Have you considered the risks and benefits associated with each strategy, and devised ways to minimize any associated dangers?

**Formulate a Customized Turnaround Plan:** Crafting a customized turnaround plan involves crafting an actionable roadmap to implement selected strategies. Your plan should take into account the resources, capabilities and limitations of your business as you craft this step-by-step roadmap.

1. What will be the core components of your turnaround plan, and how will they fit together into an effective structure?
2. Have you set measurable goals and milestones for each stage of the turnaround plan?
3. How will you ensure your plan remains flexible to adapt to unforeseen challenges or changes in the business environment?

4. What steps are being taken to include key stakeholders like employees and investors in developing and executing the turnaround plan?

**Align Leadership and Organizational Culture to Achieve Change:** A successful turnaround requires strong leadership combined with an enabling organizational culture. Make sure your leadership team is committed to your turnaround vision and prepared to lead by example, then foster an environment of innovation, open communication, and collaboration to drive its successful implementation.

1. Will you align the leadership team with the turnaround vision and ensure they are invested in its success?
2. How will you communicate the turnaround plan to employees, inspiring them to embrace change and contribute towards recovery efforts?
3. What strategies will you implement to foster innovation and cultivate a productive and resilient organizational culture?

**Implementation and Monitoring Progress:** Once your turnaround plan has been activated, its execution must be carefully and continually assessed for effectiveness. Be prepared to make necessary adjustments based on the assessment.

1. How will you ensure the turnaround strategies are implemented efficiently and effectively across all levels of the organization?
2. Which tools and metrics will you utilize to measure progress and evaluate the success of the turnaround plan?
3. How often will you review and revise the plan's milestones and performance indicators?

By crafting an effective rescue plan tailored specifically for your business, you will enable it to weather any storm and seize opportunities for growth. In our subsequent chapters, we'll examine how leadership plays a vital role in inspiring change and driving turnaround efforts - so get ready to lead it to brighter days ahead!

Now, our attention will shift towards understanding leadership's crucial role in inspiring change and driving the organization towards recovery. Effective leadership acts as the spark that ignites this journey to recovery while equipping its followers with tools for facing any obstacles along the way and looking ahead with hope toward an improved future.

**Visionary Leadership and Change Management:** Visionary leadership is at the core of successful business turnarounds. A visionary leader has the power to see beyond current obstacles and craft an attractive vision for their organization's future, inspiring and motivating their team members to embrace change with optimism, adopt new strategies with ease, and embrace any necessary adjustments that arise during transformational periods.

IBM (International Business Machines Corporation) provided a prominent example of visionary leadership during a turnaround situation during the 1990s. Facing declining profits and an ever-evolving technology landscape, CEO Louis V. Gerstner Jr. led with clarity as they transitioned away from hardware products towards software and services - leading them to achieve incredible success (source: "Who Says Elephants Can't Dance?" by Louis V. Gerstner Jr).

**Leading by Example and Fostering Trust:** A successful turnaround requires leaders who lead by example while building trust among employees and stakeholders. Leaders who demonstrate integrity, transparency, and accountability earn the respect of their teams, creating an enjoyable work environment.

An example of leading by example and building trust can be seen in the turnaround of Nissan Motor Co., Ltd. during the late 1990s. Carlos Ghosn hired to turn around this struggling automaker, demonstrated his hands-on approach and commitment to transparency with a performance evaluation system he implemented himself - earning himself the moniker "Le Cost Killer" due to his successful turnaround strategies (source: "Shift: Inside Nissan's Historic Revival" by Carlos Ghosn).

**Empowering and Engaging Employees:** When leading a turnaround, engaging employees is critical to driving transformation from within. Leaders must communicate the significance of the turnaround, include them in decision-making processes and recognize their contributions.

Ford Motor Company provided an inspiring example of employee empowerment and engagement during the Great Recession. CEO Alan Mulally engaged employees in "One Ford," his comprehensive restructuring plan designed to streamline operations and revitalize the brand, with regular "business plan review" meetings where employees from different divisions shared updates about their progress; these regular "plan review" meetings fostered a sense of ownership and collaboration across divisions - ultimately contributing to Ford's successful turnaround and resilience during tough times (source: Bryce G. Hoffman's "American Icon: Alan Mulally and His Fight to Save Ford Motor Company").

**Navigating Change and Overcoming Resistance:** Change and resisting resistance within an organization are critical components of leadership in any turnaround situation. Leaders must address employee concerns about changes, communicate the motivation behind them, provide support to facilitate their implementation, as well as resources to facilitate transitioning through any transition period that arises.

General Electric (GE), under CEO Jack Welch's guidance, provided an incredible example of successfully managing change and overcoming resistance during its turnaround in the 1980s. While many employees were resistant to his initiatives at first, Welch took them head-on by emphasizing why change was essential to secure its future - all the while emphasizing open communication and relentless commitment - ultimately leading the company's transformation into an international powerhouse (source: "Jack: Straight From The Gut" by Jack Welch).
Crisis Communication and Stakeholder Management Amid any turnaround effort, leadership must prioritize transparency and integrity when managing stakeholder concerns as well as communicating the progress and successes of their efforts to regain market dominance. Crisis Communications and Stakeholder Management

One impressive example of crisis communication and stakeholder management can be seen during British Airways (BA)'s successful turnaround in the late 1980s. Facing significant financial losses and labor disputes, CEO Colin Marshall engaged in proactive communication with employees, unions, customers and regulators. By listening and responding appropriately to each constituent group he restored employee morale and customer trust en route to a successful turnaround (source: "Flying Colours: The Inside Story of British Airways by Colin Marshall).

## Conclusion

Effective leadership is at the heart of any successful business turnaround. Visionary leaders who inspire change, lead by example, build trust and empower employees while successfully managing change can guide an organization toward recovery and growth. Examples from IBM, Nissan, Ford, GE and British Airways provide compelling proof of its transformative power during challenging times. In our next chapter, we'll delve into the critical phase of implementing rescue plans, executing identified strategies and setting a course towards revival - prepare yourself to witness its power!

# Chapter 5

## Leadership Reset: Encouraging Change and Leading Turnaround from the Top

### Introduction

This chapter highlights the essential role leadership has in successfully leading business turnaround processes. Your vision, commitment and ability to spur change as a leader are instrumental in steering your entire organization toward recovery and growth. Let's also examine transformational leadership traits as well as strategies that foster positivity and resilience during this critical stage.

**Transformational Leadership:** This goes beyond routine management; it inspires and motivates employees to achieve extraordinary results. To be an effective transformational leader, you will need to lead by example while outlining a compelling vision for the future and instilling in your team an equal sense of purpose and shared meaning.

1. How will you inspire and work together towards realizing your business's vision for transformational change?

2. How will you effectively convey the significance of recovery processes to employees so they understand their roles?

3. How will you utilize your leadership strengths to foster an environment conducive to innovation and creativity?

As a leader, your actions speak louder than words. Demonstrate your commitment to turnaround by actively participating in implementing the rescue plan and showing resilience when facing challenges; lead with integrity and transparency at all times.

1. What steps will you take to actively involve yourself in the implementation of

turnaround strategies and drive tangible results?

2. How will you exhibit resilience and positivity even when facing difficulties, encouraging your team members to adopt similar attitudes?

3. How can you promote open and honest communication among employees so they feel valued and informed throughout their experience?

**Building an Effective Leadership Team:** For successful turnaround efforts, having an enduring leadership team is paramount. Surround yourself with individuals who share your vision and bring complementary abilities.

1. How will you assess and strengthen the leadership team to meet the challenges associated with a turnaround?

2. What strategies can be implemented to encourage open communication and constructive feedback among team members to promote continuous improvement?

3. What strategies will you implement to build trust and cohesion among leadership

team members, creating a united front to lead your organization?

**Empower Employees for Change:** Engaging employees is key to any successful turnaround. Involve them in decision-making processes, recognize their contributions, and offer opportunities for skill development and growth.
1. What strategies will be put in place to include employees in the decision-making process, gathering their input and suggestions for improvement? 2. How will you recognize and reward employees for their efforts during the turnaround?
3. How will you offer training and development opportunities to upskill employees and prepare them for the challenges associated with the turnaround?

**Encourage Innovation and Adaptability:** Innovation and adaptability are essential ingredients of successful turnarounds, so foster an environment which embraces change while rewarding experimentation.

1. How will you foster an innovative culture, in which employees are encouraged to come up with fresh ideas and solutions?

2. What steps can be taken to ensure your organization remains flexible and adaptive as market dynamics and competitive landscape shift?
3. How can you foster an environment in which calculated risk-taking is encouraged and failures are seen as learning opportunities?

Assuming transformational leadership, setting an example and empowering employees are powerful methods for cultivating a positive and resilient culture which is necessary for the successful execution of any turnaround plan. We will explore in greater depth in Chapter 2, how important it is to form a high-performing turnaround team aligned around shared goals; so rally your troops and build one!

Now, our attention must shift to the critical task of implementing our rescue plan successfully; this chapter outlines strategies and key elements necessary to effectively implement turnaround initiatives and set the stage for its revival.

**Formulate a Roadmap for Execution Establishing an Execution Roadmap:** To implement a rescue plan effectively requires creating a clearly-outlined execution roadmap that outlines all actions, timelines, responsibilities and performance indicators necessary. This roadmap serves as a guide for the organization while assuring all stakeholders remain aligned during the execution process.

One real-life example of successful turnaround execution through an established roadmap is The Boeing Company. After suffering significant delays and issues with their Dreamliner 787 program, Boeing appointed Jim McNerney as CEO and implemented a detailed execution plan involving engineering teams, suppliers, regulatory bodies and more - ultimately successfully overcoming technical challenges related to Dreamliner production (source: "Boeing Versus Airbus: The Inside Story of the Greatest International Competition in Business by John Newhouse).

**Allocating Resources and Prioritizing Initiatives:** A successful turnaround relies upon effective resource allocation. Financial, human, and technological resources should be allocated strategically towards initiatives with the greatest impact for recovery.

Netflix Inc. in the mid-2000s provided an illuminating example of resource allocation and prioritization during a turnaround when CEO Reed Hastings recognized streaming technology's potential and used his resources to build out its streaming platform despite initial opposition from some stakeholders; as a result, a dramatic transformation occurred within Netflix's business model that led to DVD rental becoming obsolete, leading to its dominance of entertainment industry (source: "No Rules Rules: Netflix and the Culture of Reinvention by Reed Hastings and Erin Meyer).

**Effective Project Management and Accountability:** Effective project management is essential to ensuring turnaround initiatives stay on course and are completed within their set timelines. Assigning clear accountability to individuals and teams fosters ownership and responsibility for its successful execution.

FCA was transformed under CEO Sergio Marchionne with an effective project management and accountability program called World Class Manufacturing (WCM), designed to increase efficiency and quality across operations while creating a culture of accountability among employees responsible for continuous improvement initiatives. WCM played an instrumental role in FCA's turnaround and return to profitability (source: "Leadership in Organizations" by Gary A. Yukl).

**Monitoring Progress and Being Flexible in Execution:** It is key for companies during turnarounds to remain flexible in execution and adapt quickly to changing circumstances. Reviewing key performance indicators (KPIs) regularly is an effective way for leaders to identify any potential hurdles early and make informed decisions.

As an illustration of progress measurement and adaptability in execution, consider the turnaround of Xerox Corporation under CEO Anne Mulcahy. Facing serious financial difficulties during the early 2000s, Mulcahy implemented a turnaround plan with continuous monitoring of KPIs and frequent reviews of strategies; through this flexibility of execution, Xerox made adjustments necessary to achieve recovery (source: David Kiley's "How Xerox Came Back From the Dead", BusinessWeek).

**Empowering Employees and Fostering a Culture of Change:** A successful turnaround requires empowering and motivating employees, while leaders must establish an environment which welcomes change while encouraging employees to take ownership over their roles in transformation processes. An outstanding real-life example of empowering employees and fostering change can be seen during Microsoft Corporation's transformation under CEO Satya Nadella. Under his guidance, Microsoft adopted a culture which valued innovation, agility, employee empowerment and taking risks with no consequences; encouraging employees to experiment without fear. This shift proved vital in Microsoft's successful turnaround and its subsequent re-emergence as a technology industry leader (source: "Hit Refresh: The Quest to Rediscover Microsoft's Soul and Imagine a Better Future for All by Satya Nadella).

## Conclusion

Implementing a rescue plan is central to any successful business turnaround strategy. Successful turnaround implementation relies upon creating an action plan for implementation, allocating resources wisely, practicing effective project management techniques, monitoring progress reports, engaging employees in change initiatives and cultivating an atmosphere conducive to change. These factors must come together seamlessly in order to be achieved successfully. Real-life examples such as those seen at Boeing, Netflix, Fiat Chrysler Automobiles, Xerox and Microsoft show the transformative power of effective execution during tough times. We will explore in Chapter Three the essential role collaboration and teamwork play in helping organizations recover quickly and position them for an optimistic future. Prepare yourself to experience collective effort and synergy at work!

# Chapter 6
## Rallying the Troops: Assembling a High-Performing Turnaround Team

In this chapter, we addressed the importance of creating an efficient turnaround team to execute rescue plans effectively. A skilled and motivated team is essential in successfully managing business turnaround challenges while driving an organization towards brighter prospects. Let's identify key members to include on such teams as well as strategies that foster an environment conducive to their success.

**Finding Key Players:** The key to any successful turnaround lies in building the right team. Recognize key roles essential for recovery such as financial experts, marketing specialists, operational managers and change management experts.
1. Who are the key members you should include on your turnaround team, and what expertise do they offer?
2. How will you establish clear role definitions and responsibilities within the

team to reduce overlapped efforts or potential conflicts between members?

**Skill Assessment and Development:** Conduct a detailed evaluation of every team member's skills and competencies, noting any skill gaps that need addressing in order to ensure your team can successfully tackle challenges ahead.

1. How will you assess the skills and competencies of each team member to identify areas for improvement?
2. Which strategies will be implemented to provide training and development opportunities so as to bolster the skill set of your team?

**Foster Team Collaboration to make teams more effective**

An effective team is essential in meeting complex challenges head-on. Foster an environment in which team members work closely together, share knowledge, and support each other.

1. How will you foster open communication and constructive feedback among team members in order to foster collaboration?
2. Which activities/workshops will be organized in order to strengthen bonds among team members?

**Setting Clear Goals and Expectations:** To ensure team efforts are aligned, set clear goals and expectations for every member. Make sure everyone understands their roles in the turnaround and the impact of their contributions.

1. How will you communicate the overall goals and individual contributions related to the turnaround to the team, while attuning to individual responsibilities within this goal?
2. Will measures be put in place to track progress while holding all team members accountable?

Empower the Team Enable your team members to take responsibility for their tasks and make decisions that contribute to the turnaround's success.

1. How will you encourage team members to take initiative and make decisions aligned with turnaround objectives?
2. Which strategies will you employ to recognize and reward team members' efforts and achievements?

**Handling Team Challenges:** Identify any possible team challenges and develop strategies to effectively deal with them quickly.

1. What steps will be taken to address conflicts or disagreements within your team in order to create an optimal working environment?
2. How will you boost team morale and motivation during challenging periods?

Continuous Learning and Improvement Foster a culture of continuous learning and improvement within your team by emphasizing its importance in adapting strategies based on feedback or changing circumstances.

1. How will you foster an environment of learning and innovation, where team members are encouraged to experiment and

adapt their approaches? 2. What methods are in place for gathering feedback from team members so you can evaluate the success of turnaround strategies?

Build a high-performing turnaround team and foster an atmosphere of cooperation and support to enable your organization to overcome obstacles and meet goals outlined in its rescue plan. In the next chapter, we'll look at the essential role cash flow management plays during crises; its effect can have on survival and recovery strategies; prepare to secure its financial wellbeing!

Now, our attention will turn towards collaboration and teamwork as key ingredients of organizational recovery during business turnarounds. Collaboration among employees and stakeholders can lead to positive transformation that propels an organization toward an optimistic future.

Fostering a Collaborative Culture: To ensure successful turnaround efforts, leaders must foster an environment which fosters open communication, mutual respect, and the free flow of ideas between team members.

Pixar Animation Studios stands as a prime example of how to foster a collaborative culture. Under the leadership of Ed Catmull and Steve Jobs, Pixar became an animation powerhouse by emphasizing collaboration among creative talent. Cross-functional teams were encouraged to work on projects together while an "Braintrust" of creative leaders provided constructive feedback for films in development - ultimately leading to blockbuster movies being produced at Pixar (source: "Creativity Inc." by Ed Catmull).

**Breaking Down Silos and Departmental Barriers:** In any turnaround scenario, breaking down silos and departmental barriers is crucial to align efforts toward the common goal of recovery. Cross-functional collaboration helps facilitate knowledge sharing between departments as well as providing innovative solutions for problems at hand.

Johnson & Johnson (J&J) serves as an excellent example of breaking down silos and encouraging collaboration. Confronted by product quality issues and public relations challenges, J&J implemented the "One J&J" initiative - designed to unify various divisions within their organization while encouraging collaboration to address common challenges.

J&J's recovery benefited greatly from this collaborative approach and reinforced its dedication to improving healthcare worldwide (Source: "Johnson & Johnson's One J&J Initiative", by Dan Ciampa and Michael Watkins of Harvard Business Review).
Empowering Teams and Encouraging Ownership: During a turnaround, empowering teams and encouraging ownership are crucial for driving results. Leaders must assign responsibilities accordingly so that teams take charge in taking control of their roles in the transformation process.

One powerful real-life example of team empowerment and encouraging ownership can be seen in The LEGO Group's turnaround. When faced with financial challenges in the early 2000s, LEGO launched the "Workout" initiative involving cross-functional teams tasked with evaluating and improving specific aspects of its business. By engaging their employees through these teams, LEGO leveraged their creativity and expertise for product innovation as well as financial recovery (source: "Brick by Brick: How LEGO Rewrote the Rules of Innovation and Conquered the Global Toy Industry", by David Robertson & Bill Breen).

Promotion of Communication and Knowledge Sharing Communication and knowledge sharing are integral to teamwork during any turnaround, and leaders must make sure information flows freely so teams can make informed decisions and align their efforts effectively.

IBM (International Business Machines Corporation) serves as an excellent example of effective communication and knowledge-sharing during a turnaround. CEO Louis V. Gerstner Jr. initiated "Worldwide Management Briefings," where executives from different regions and divisions exchanged best practices and shared information, which allowed IBM to leverage global expertise while strengthening team collaboration resulting in its successful turnaround (Source: "Who Says Elephants Can't Dance?" by Louis V. Gerstner Jr).

**Rewarding Team Achievements at Turnaround:** Recognizing and rewarding team achievements during a turnaround can bolster collective effort while building morale. Acknowledging individual and collective contributions promotes feelings of pride and camaraderie among employees.

At Verizon Communications, one real-life example of how to recognize team achievements during a turnaround can be seen with their "Verizon Communications' Spotlight Awards" by Anne Morriss and Frances X Frei (Harvard Business Review). They offered employees a recognition program dubbed the "Spotlight Award." Employees could nominate colleagues or teams they felt made significant contributions towards turning around operations - this played an instrumental role in motivating employees while strengthening collaboration (source: "Verizon Communications' Spotlight Awards" by Anne Morriss and Frances X Frei in Harvard Business Review).

**Conclusion**

Collaboration and teamwork are cornerstones of business turnaround success. By creating a collaborative culture, breaking down silos, empowering teams, promoting communication, and recognising achievements a powerful synergy is created that propels organizations toward recovery and growth. Examples from Pixar, Johnson & Johnson, The LEGO Group, IBM and Verizon illustrate its transformative effect during challenging times. In the next chapter we'll cover how sustaining turnaround success through long-term growth resilience strategies will ensure business survival after transformation takes place! So get ready to secure its future while embarking upon this path of transformation!

# Chapter 7
## Cash is King: Handling Liquidity in Times of Crisis

This chapter addresses the critical nature of managing finances and liquidity during a business turnaround. As "cash is king", its availability becomes essential to maintaining operations, meeting obligations, investing in recovery efforts, and staying afloat financially. Let's examine strategies to optimize cash flow while cutting unnecessary expenses to maintain financial security for your enterprise.

**Establishing Cash Flow:** To begin, conduct a comprehensive examination of your business's cash flow. Analyze inflows and outflows carefully to identify any bottlenecks or cash traps.

1. How will you evaluate the current cash flow situation, and which key financial metrics will you analyze?
2. Have any cash flow patterns or trends that require immediate attention or improvement emerged

**Optimizing Receivables and Payables:** Streamlining your accounts receivable and payable processes can dramatically affect cash flow. Explore strategies to shorten payment cycles or extend payment terms wherever possible.

1. How will you speed up the collection of outstanding receivables to increase cash inflow? 2. What measures will be implemented to negotiate favorable payment terms with suppliers without straining relationships?

**Controlling Costs and Expenses:** In the face of an economic recession, cost control becomes paramount. Review all expenses to identify where cost-cutting measures may be applied without jeopardizing product or service quality.

1. How will you conduct a cost analysis to identify non-essential expenses that can be reduced or eliminated?
2. Which strategies will you implement to ensure cost-cutting measures do not negatively affect employee morale and customer experience?

**Inventory Optimization:** Inventory management is key to cash flow optimization. Aim for an equilibrium between maintaining sufficient stock levels to satisfy customer demands and avoiding overstock that ties up cash resources.

1. How will you assess current inventory levels to ensure they align with demand projections?
2. What steps are being taken to implement just-in-time inventory practices to minimize excess stock and associated holding costs?

**Negotiate With Creditors and Lenders:** During a turnaround, communication with creditors and lenders becomes critical. Be upfront about your company's challenges while exploring whether renegotiating payment terms or seeking additional funding might be an option.

1. What strategies will be implemented to foster cooperation from creditors and lenders during a turnaround process? 2. If necessary, which tactics will you utilize in order to negotiate favorable loan terms or access additional credit lines if needed?

**Emergency Funding Solutions:** When traditional financing sources are unavailable, explore alternative emergency funding sources, such as asset-based financing, factoring or crowdfunding.

1. How will you evaluate and manage risks associated with various emergency funding options? 2. What steps are necessary to secure emergency funding without jeopardizing the long-term financial health of the business?

**Cash Flow Forecasting:** Employ effective cash flow forecasting practices to gain clarity into future cash requirements and anticipate any potential challenges that might arise.

1. How will you create a cash flow forecast that takes into account various scenarios and variables that could impede on your business?
2. At what frequency will you review and update the cash flow forecast to account for changes in the business environment?

By efficiently overseeing finances and liquidity, your business will gain the financial strength to withstand stormy times while executing turnaround strategies outlined in its rescue plan. In our next chapter, we'll examine how winning back customers and restoring trust are essential parts of this turnaround process - get ready to regain market trust!

Now, our attention turns towards maintaining business success post-turnaround. In this chapter, we outlined the strategies and key elements necessary for long-term growth and resilience within an organization.

**Create a Vision for the Future**

Sustaining success begins with creating a clear vision for the future. A well-defined vision gives an organization a sense of direction and purpose, providing guidance in its actions and decisions.
Satya Nadella of Microsoft Corporation serves as an excellent example of crafting a compelling vision for its future. After becoming CEO, Nadella articulated a compelling vision focused on empowering every individual and organization through technology to realize more success; this guided their transformation to becoming a

cloud-first mobile-first company as well as sustained growth and innovation (Sources: Official Microsoft website and "Hit Refresh: The Quest to Rediscover Microsoft's Soul and Imagine a Better Future for Everyone by Satya Nadella).

**Innovation for Market Relevance**

Organizations must embrace innovation and adapt to changing market dynamics to sustain their success. Doing so allows businesses to remain relevant and competitive in an ever-evolving landscape.

Amazon.com Inc. is an excellent example of continuous innovation to maintain market relevance. Under founder and CEO Jeff Bezos' guidance, Amazon introduced numerous ground breaking products and services like Prime, Kindle, and AWS (Amazon Web Services). By consistently innovating new offerings into new markets and diversifying revenue sources through expansion (source: "The Everything Store: Jeff Bezos and the Age of Amazon", by Brad Stone).

**Investment in Human Capital**

Sustaining success requires investing in human capital to build an experienced, motivated, and engaged workforce. Leaders must prioritize employee development, engagement, and well-being for ongoing growth.

Google (now Alphabet Inc.), with its highly renowned work culture and employee-friendly policies, invests heavily in employee development. They also offer attractive benefits. Google's focus on human capital has contributed significantly to attracting top talent and creating an innovative culture within their ranks (source: "Work Rules!: Insights from Inside Google That Will Transform How You Live and Lead", written by Laszlo Bock).

**Building a Resilient Business Model**

Resilient business models are essential in order to withstand economic fluctuations and disruptive forces, so organizations must regularly evaluate their models in order to identify areas for improvement and adapt to new challenges.

The Walt Disney Company serves as an excellent example of creating a resilient business model. Disney was able to successfully adapt their business model in response to changing consumer behaviors and technological advancements by adopting streaming services and direct-to-consumer content distribution (source: "The Ride of a Lifetime: Lessons Learned from 15 Years as CEO of the Walt Disney Company" by Robert Iger).

**Customers-Centric Approach**

Maintaining a customer-focused approach is the cornerstone of long-term success for any organization. Businesses must listen carefully to feedback from their customers, anticipate their needs and deliver products and services that offer them both value and exceptional experiences.

Zappos stands as an outstanding example of an organization taking a customer-centric approach, known for their outstanding customer service and commitment to customer satisfaction. By cultivating long-term relationships with its customers, they were able to achieve sustainable growth with increased brand loyalty (source:

"Delivering Happiness: A Path to Profits, Passion and Purpose" by Tony Hsieh).

**Strategic Partnerships and Alliances**

Organizations seeking long-term growth should form strategic alliances and partnerships that leverage each other's strengths and broaden market coverage. Starbucks Corporation and Nestle S.A are an example of strategic partnerships. Starbucks formed a global coffee alliance with Nestle to expand their distribution channels and bring Starbucks products to new markets, while this agreement allowed both firms to leverage each other's expertise and customer bases resulting in mutual growth (source: Starbucks Corporation press release).

**Conclusion**

To sustain success beyond a turnaround requires taking an integrated approach that positions the organization for long-term growth and resilience. By creating a clear vision, fostering innovation, investing in human capital, developing a resilient business model that puts customers first, and forging strategic partnerships, organizations can thrive in an ever-evolving business landscape. Real-life examples from Microsoft, Amazon, Google, Disney, Zappos, Starbucks and Nestle show the transformative impact of business turnaround strategies on sustained success. We will look back on this journey of business turnaround with valuable lessons learned - get ready for continuous growth and success as you embrace this art form!

# Chapter 8
## Regaining Customer Trust and Loyalty

Customers are the foundation of any business's growth and success; here, we examine strategies to reconnect with your customer base, address their concerns, and regain their trust.

**Customer Feedback and Insights (CFAI)**

Gather feedback from your customers in order to identify their needs, expectations and pain points. Examine customer interactions such as surveys or online reviews in order to identify areas for improvement.

1. How will you collect and analyze customer feedback to gain insights into customer perceptions of your products or services?
2. Have any recurring issues or patterns been identified which must be addressed during the turnaround?

Once identified, once customer concerns have been identified promptly address them through developing action plans that address customer issues and enhance overall customer experience.

1. How will you communicate with customers to keep them apprised of steps taken to address their complaints? 2. Which strategies will be employed in providing timely and effective solutions to customer problems?
3. Winning Customers Back
Rebuilding Brand Trust Establishing trust in your brand is crucial to winning back customers, so transparency, consistency,

and delivering on promises should be at the core of regaining customer confidence.

1. How will you communicate your commitment to transparency and honesty in all business dealings?
2. Which measures have been implemented to ensure consistent delivery of products or services that meet or surpass customer expectations?

**Personalized Customer Engagement:** Tailor your customer engagement strategies to offer each of your customers an individualized experience by leveraging data and insights to anticipate their needs and preferences.

1. How will you leverage customer data to provide tailored recommendations and promotions?
2. Which strategies can strengthen emotional connections between your brand and customers?

**Encourage Repeat Business By Offering Incentives and Loyalty Programs:** Provide incentives and loyalty programs as rewards to existing customers to encourage repeat purchases.

1. How will you design loyalty programs or incentives that enhance customer experiences? 2. What steps will be taken to effectively communicate these programs' advantages to customers?

**Communicate Effectively and Market Successfully:** Create captivating marketing messages that highlight improvements and changes made during a turnaround, using channels that effectively reach target audiences.

1. How will the business develop marketing campaigns to reflect its commitment to change and improvement?
2. Have you identified suitable communication channels to reach target audiences?

**Deliver a Consistent Brand Experience:** It is crucial that your brand provides a consistent experience across all touchpoints, from online presence to physical store interactions, in order to foster brand loyalty.

1. How will all customer touchpoints reflect your brand values and promises?
2. Which strategies will ensure an enjoyable customer journey throughout your turnaround process?

You can lay the groundwork for renewed growth and long-term success by prioritising customer acquisition and rebuilding trust in your brand. In our next chapter, we'll explore how innovation and adaptability play an integral part in driving business turnaround and positioning you for future success. Get ready to embrace change while staying ahead of the game!

This chapter delves deeper into these invaluable experiences for guidance and inspiration for further endeavors.

**Accepting Change as an Unchangeable Force**

One of the key lessons from business turnarounds is understanding that change is an inevitable component of doing business. Market dynamics, consumer preferences and technological advances all play a role, necessitating organizations to be agile and adaptive to adapt quickly to evolving conditions.

One tangible example of accepting change as a constant can be seen in Nokia Corporation. Once dominant in the mobile phone industry, Nokia found itself struggling as smartphones became a common trend. Although initially slow to adapt, Nokia eventually recognized the need for change and formed a strategic partnership with Microsoft using Windows Phone operating system - yet even this transformation wasn't enough to restore former glory (Source: "The Decline and Fall of Nokia by David J. Cord).

**Resilience in the Face of Adversity**

Business turnarounds teach us the value of resilience in the face of hardship. Successful organizations demonstrate this trait by being able to adapt quickly to challenges, learn from failures and persevere during trying times.

IBM (International Business Machines Corporation) stands as an excellent example of resilience in business turnaround. Beginning in the early 1990s, due to a decline in mainframe computer sales, IBM faced financial strain and went through significant restructuring under CEO Louis V. Gerstner Jr. The transformation took some time; however, through resilience and dedication to change it ultimately led to its resurgence (Source: "Who Says Elephants Can't Dance?" by Louis V. Gerstner Jr).

**Adopt a Customer-Centric Approach**

Customer-centric mindsets are of utmost importance during turnaround scenarios. Businesses that prioritize customer needs, preferences and feedback gain a competitive advantage while forging customer loyalty.
Domino's Pizza Inc. provides an example of successfully adopting a customer-centric mindset. After receiving feedback about the quality of pizza, it underwent an immense brand transformation by listening to customer comments, revamping recipes, and initiating an advertising campaign which candidly acknowledged past shortcomings - leading to higher customer satisfaction levels and ultimately higher sales (Source: "Pizza Tiger" by Tom Monaghan and Robert Anderson).

**Learning From Failure and Adaptation**

Turnaround efforts often involve experiencing setbacks and failures, offering important lessons that lead to adaptation and improved strategies.
Learning from Failure and Adaptation One prominent example of learning from failure and adaptation is Burberry Group plc's turnaround in the early 2000s. While dealing with issues surrounding counterfeiting of its brand image, under Angela Ahrendts and Christopher Bailey the company repositioned its brand by investing heavily in digital marketing and innovation (e.g. investing in digital marketing campaigns to maintain global growth; Lauren Sherman of Business of Fashion wrote up this story about this). As a result of its adaptation to digital environments, it saw increased brand appeal and global expansion (source "Burberry Turns To Digital Luxury" by Lauren Sherman at Business of Fashion).

**Innovation for Sustainable Growth**

Sustainable growth demands continuous innovation and an eagerness to explore new possibilities. Businesses that invest in R&D

and embrace innovation are poised for long-term success.

Apple Inc. is an excellent example of innovating to achieve sustained growth. Under Steve Jobs' visionary leadership, they introduced revolutionary products such as iPod, iPhone and iPad that revolutionized respective markets while positioning Apple as one of the leading technology companies (source: "Steve Jobs" by Walter Isaacson).

**Conclusion**

The transformative journey of business turnaround offers invaluable lessons that can assist organizations during times of crises and uncertainty. Adopting change as an inevitable constant, showing resilience against obstacles, adopting a customer-focused mindset, learning from failure and encouraging innovation are essential ingredients of a successful turnaround. Real-life examples from Nokia, IBM, Domino's Pizza, Burberry and Apple demonstrate the significance of lessons from these real-life examples in achieving sustained business success. When embarking on business turnaround strategies, remember that every challenge represents an opportunity for growth and improvement; may these lessons serve as beacons of inspiration in your pursuit of excellence in this dynamic world of business.

# Chapter 9

## Reinventing for Long-Term Success

This chapter investigates the essential role that innovation and adaptability play in driving business turnaround and positioning it for long-term success. With today's ever-evolving business landscape, being flexible enough to innovate is necessary in staying relevant and competitive - let's delve into strategies for cultivating an environment of innovation while welcoming change and taking advantage of new opportunities for growth.

**Cultivating an Environment of Innovation:** Develop an environment that fosters creativity, experimentation and continuous improvement. Empower employees with their ideas while offering them a safe space to think creatively.

1. How will you promote innovation as a core value within the organization?
2. Which strategies will be put in place to recognize and reward innovative ideas from employees?

**Discovering Growth Opportunities**

1. How will your organization conduct market research to identify unexploited growth opportunities?
2. Which steps will be taken to evaluate and verify these growth opportunities?

**Consider Forming Strategic Partnerships or Alliances:** Explore entering into strategic partnerships or alliances with other businesses to leverage their expertise, access new markets or technologies, access potential new partners, and evaluate any benefits of forging alliances.

One question to address when considering this path forward:

1. How will you identify potential alliance partners and evaluate any associated benefits?
2. What measures will be put in place to ensure successful collaboration and mutual value creation?

**Staying Current with Technological Advancements:** It's essential that businesses stay current with technological innovations that could disrupt their industry, adopting new technologies to increase operational efficiencies and enhance customer experiences.
1. How will you track technological trends and assess their potential impact on your business?
2. Which strategies will be implemented to adopt and integrate new technologies effectively?

**Agile Decision-Making and Resource Allocation:** Implement a rapid decision-making process that provides quick responses to market changes. Allocate resources efficiently for innovation and growth initiatives.

1. How will you streamline decision-making processes to enable faster responses to market shifts?
2. What measures will be implemented to allocate resources effectively in support of innovation and adaptation?

**Innovation and Risk Management Strategies:** To promote calculated risks while efficiently mitigating any potential ones, devise risk management plans to protect businesses during periods of innovation.
1. How will you foster an environment in which calculated risk-taking is encouraged and failures are seen as learning experiences?
2. Which measures will you implement to manage risks associated with innovative initiatives?

**Acceptance and Continuous Improvement**
1. How will you communicate the importance of change and continuous improvement to employees?
2. Which strategies will be employed to ensure that the organization can adapt quickly to changing market conditions?

Your business can become better prepared to navigate the complexities of today's business landscape by cultivating a culture of innovation, welcoming change and seizing growth opportunities. In our next chapter, we'll examine the role effective communication has during a turnaround process and its effect on employee engagement and stakeholder support - so be ready to communicate clearly and inspire action!

# Chapter 10

## Thriving Amid Uncertainty: Establishing a Culture of Continuous Improvement

Introduction

Over the past chapters, we explored key components of a successful business turnaround, including visionary leadership, creating the rescue plan, executing strategies, fostering collaboration and reflecting on valuable lessons learned. Now as we near the conclusion of our journey, we examine the significance of creating a culture of continuous improvement; organizations must embrace innovation and adaptability with commitment to long-term growth in order to thrive over time.

**Accepting and Adopting a Growth Mindset**

Building a culture of continuous improvement begins with adopting a growth mindset across your organization. A growth mindset promotes belief in one's own potential to improve and understand that abilities can be developed with dedication and hard work.

One real-life example of adopting a growth mindset can be seen through Microsoft Corporation's journey under CEO Satya Nadella. Under Nadella's guidance, Microsoft underwent a cultural transformation that prioritized adopting this type of thinking among employees. He encouraged employees to embrace change, learn from failures, and pursue opportunities for personal and professional growth - something which ultimately contributed to their successful turnaround as they evolved into becoming cloud-first mobile-first (Sources include their official website as well as Satya Nadella's book Hit

Refresh: The Quest to Rediscover Microsoft's Soul and Imagine a Better Future For All by Satya Nadella).

## Fostering Employee-Led Innovation at Your Workplace

Within an environment of continuous improvement, employees are encouraged to be creative and contribute ideas that promote positive change. When employees take ownership of innovation they feel more motivated in their work and achieve a sense of fulfillment and purpose through it.
3M Company stands as an excellent example of employee-led innovation. Their culture encourages employees to spend 15% of their workday exploring innovative ideas - which has resulted in iconic products like Post-it Notes and Scotch Tape being created as a result. By rewarding employee creativity, 3M has maintained its competitive edge and sustained long-term growth (source: "Post-it Note Mogul: How 3M's Legendary Invention Manager Sparked a Revolution", by Geoffrey A. Fowler published by The Wall Street Journal).

**Establishing a Learning Organization**

Organizations can foster an environment of continuous improvement when they become learning organizations. Such companies prioritize knowledge sharing and employee development to stay abreast with industry advancements.
General Electric (GE) stands as an excellent example of an organization that successfully created a learning organization under CEO Jack Welch's guidance. Through the "Work-Out" program, they implemented process improvements that increased efficiency and profitability (source: "Control Your Destiny or Someone Else Will" by Noel M. Tichy and Stratford Sherman).

**Decision-Making Based on Data**

Data-driven decision-making is integral to an environment of continuous improvement, and organizations must rely on data analytics and insights to guide their strategic choices and identify areas for enhancement. Netflix Inc. is an excellent example of data-driven decision-making, employing data analysis to gain an in-depth understanding of customer preferences and viewing habits, informing their content creation, recommendation algorithms and user experience as part of their success (reference: Gina Keating's "Netflixed: The Epic Battle for America's Eyeballs").

**Encourage Feedback and Adaptation (IFFA)**

To foster continuous improvement, organizations must encourage feedback and be willing to change. By seeking input from employees, customers, and stakeholders alike, businesses can identify areas for enhancement as well as any deficiencies.
Toyota Motor Corporation serves as an ideal example of encouraging feedback and adaptation through its "Kaizen" philosophy, which promotes continuous improvement through small changes based on input from employees and customers alike. This approach has contributed significantly to Toyota's success and earned them recognition for quality and innovation (source: "The Toyota Way: 14 Management Principles from the World's Greatest Manufacturer," by Jeffrey K. Liker).

## Conclusion

For businesses navigating an unpredictable business landscape, creating a culture of continuous improvement is key to remaining successful amid uncertainty. An effective culture involves adopting a growth mindset, encouraging employee-led innovation, building a learning organization and practicing data-driven decision-making; these components should all play an integral role. Feedback and adaptation should also be promoted. Real-world examples from Microsoft, 3M, GE, Netflix and Toyota illustrate the transformative impact of these principles on sustained success. As you conclude the journey of business turnaround, remember that continuous improvement should be an ongoing effort of excellence and growth. Be open to change, innovation and the spirit of continuous improvement to ensure long-term success for your organization in today's ever-evolving global business arena.

# Chapter 11

## Harnessing Transparent Messaging in Times of Crisis

In this chapter, we explored the significance of effective communication in business turnaround processes. Transparent and clear messaging is key to maintaining stakeholder confidence, encouraging employee engagement, securing investor and partner support and forging bonds during times of crisis. Let's explore strategies for creating engaging communication that addresses all stakeholder's concerns while building trust during an upheaval.

**Crafting a Communication Strategy:** It is critical that companies create a comprehensive communications strategy in line with their turnaround objectives, taking into account all stakeholders (such as employees, customers, investors, suppliers and the wider community) as part of this plan.

1. What will you use to identify the communication needs of various stakeholder groups?

2. Which channels will effectively deliver your messages to each stakeholder group?

**Be Open and Honest When Communicating**: Be upfront and forthcoming when discussing challenges faced by your business and honest about the steps being taken to address them. Openness builds trust while showing commitment towards finding solutions.

1. How will you communicate the current state and need for turnaround of the business to stakeholders and other necessary individuals/agencies?

2. Are any measures planned to ensure consistency in messaging across all communication channels?

**Employee Engagement and Communication:** Engage employees in the turnaround process and keep them apprised of its progress. Employees who understand an organization's goals and challenges are more likely to be motivated and supportive.

1. How will you involve employees in decision-making processes, solicit their input

and utilize effective communication strategies to keep employees updated on the status of the turnaround?

**Anticipate and Respond to Stakeholder Concerns:** Anticipate and address the concerns of various stakeholders. Provide answers promptly and clearly when responding to inquiries or feedback.
1. How will you proactively address investors, customers, suppliers, or any other key players?
2. What steps will you take to ensure stakeholders receive timely and accurate information?

**Establish Trust and Credibility:** Consistently, transparent communication helps build trust with stakeholders. Establish yourself as reliable and accountable by creating an image of reliability.
1. What steps will you take to demonstrate consistency and credibility in your communications efforts?
2. What strategies will be implemented to rebuild trust with stakeholders who may have been adversely impacted by your business's challenges?

**Manage Public Perception:** A crisis can have a profound effect on public perception, so be proactive in managing PR to foster positive narratives about your business and address any negative perceptions or misinformation surrounding its turnaround process. 1 How will you address negative perceptions or misinformation related to it during its turnaround process?

2. What measures will be taken to inform the public of your turnaround's progress and achievements?

**Monitoring and Evaluating Communication Effectiveness:** KPMG assess the success of your communication efforts regularly by collecting feedback from stakeholders and monitoring key performance indicators.

1. How will you gather feedback from stakeholders to assess the effect of your communication strategy?

2. Which metrics will be used to assess the success of your communications efforts?

Utilising transparent messaging and effective communication will enable you to build stakeholder support, strengthen employee engagement and position your business for successful recovery and expansion. In our final chapter, we'll celebrate your accomplishments during this transformation and explore strategies to maintain its success over time - let's celebrate!

**Promoting an Environment of Adaptability to Promote Long-term Resilience**

As discussed in previous chapters, business turnaround requires many essential elements, from visionary leadership and crafting the rescue plan, executing strategies, fostering collaboration, and reflecting on valuable lessons, to building a culture of continuous improvement. Now we look towards our final destination of cultivating an adaptive culture. In an age of unprecedented disruption and uncertainty, organizations must build resilience as quickly as possible in order to maintain long-term success.

**Understanding Adaptability Needs in Organizations**

Establishing an adaptable culture begins with acknowledging the necessity of change early. Organizations should recognize that market conditions, consumer behavior and technological innovations may rapidly alter over time requiring swift responses in order to remain relevant.

Adobe Systems Incorporated provides an excellent example of adaptability at work: in response to declining revenues from traditional software sales, they recognized and responded swiftly to the shift toward subscription-based services and cloud computing by successfully transitioning their business model by offering Creative Cloud subscriptions - thus guaranteeing their place as leaders of the creative software industry (source: "The Story of Adobe Systems Incorporated by Max Buxton).

## Agility in Decision-Making

An adaptable culture requires swift decision-making. Organizations must quickly evaluate opportunities and risks, before taking informed, timely decisions that reflect these assessments.

Nike Inc. is an example of agility when it comes to decision-making. During the COVID-19 pandemic, they quickly changed their strategy by shifting focus toward digital sales and e-commerce to respond to changing consumer behavior - thus mitigating store closure impacts while maintaining market position (source: Angelica LaVito's article "Inside Nike's Decision to Kick Amazon to the Curb", CNBC).

**Promoting a Growth Mindset at All Levels:** To foster adaptability, organizations must foster a growth mindset across all levels. Employees should be encouraged to embrace change, take calculated risks and perceive challenges as opportunities for personal and professional development.
LinkedIn Corporation serves as an outstanding example of cultivating a growth mindset. Employees at the company are encouraged to pursue projects outside their typical roles and foster an environment of continual learning and adaptability that has produced products and services tailored specifically to its user base (source: "LinkedIn's CEO on Adaptability", Ryan Roslansky of Harvard Business Review).

**Resilience in Times of Crises**

Building an adaptive culture also demands resilience when crisis hits. Organizations must face these obstacles with optimism and be open to learning from any setbacks that arise.

Resilience in times of crisis was illustrated by Best Buy Co., Inc.'s turnaround strategy during their "Renew Blue" transformation strategy in response to increased competition and online retailer growth. Focusing on improving in-store experiences, increasing online sales and optimizing supply chains; Best Buy was able to outwit what had become known as "retail apocalypse", returning as one of the leaders of consumer electronics (source: "The End of Best Buy?" by Adam Lashinsky of Fortune).

## Continued Innovation and Market Sensing are Key Components for Success

Enhancing adaptability requires organizations to be constantly innovative and follow market trends, being responsive to consumer preferences changes and emerging technologies. Organizations should remain vigilant in sensing any shifts that might affect them and take proactive measures against unexpected situations that might arise.

Spotify Technology S.A is an example of continuous innovation and market sensing at work, as seen in their highly competitive music streaming industry. They consistently introduce new features and personalized playlists to meet user preferences - keeping pace with competitors while remaining one of the leading music streaming platforms (source: Spotify's official website).

**Conclusion**

Cultivating an adaptability culture is vital to ensuring long-term resilience in today's ever-evolving business landscape. Understanding the necessity for adaptability, agility in decision-making, cultivating a growth mindset, being resilient in times of crisis, continuous innovation and market sensing are essential components of an ideal corporate culture. Real-life examples from Adobe, Nike, LinkedIn, Best Buy and Spotify show the transformative impact of adaptability on sustained success. As you complete the transformative journey of business turnaround, keep adaptability at the center of resilience and long-term success - embrace change, embrace innovation and embrace adaptability's spirit in order to future-proof your organization in today's dynamic business environment.

# Chapter 12

## Emerging Stronger: Recognizing Success and Sustaining Turnaround

### Introduction

In this final chapter, we recognize the achievements made during business turnaround and discuss strategies to maintain its success long-term. A successful turnaround marks a new chapter for your company and building on that momentum is essential to its continued growth and resilience.

### Review of Turnaround Journey

Take the time to reflect upon the challenges encountered, strategies implemented and progress made during your turnaround process. Be sure to recognize your team's efforts and any support from stakeholders who assisted in its success.

1. How will you honor your team's achievements and show appreciation to key stakeholders during the turnaround journey?
2. What lessons did you take away from this experience, and how will they apply in future endeavors?

**Maintaining Turnaround Momentum**

Now is the time to capitalize on and sustain all the positive changes implemented during the turnaround process.

1. What strategies will be implemented to sustain the positive changes brought about during your turnaround?
2. How will you ensure that the business remains flexible and adaptable enough to face future challenges and opportunities?

**Continuous Innovation and improvement**

Create and foster an environment of continuous improvement and innovation, accepting change as an ongoing feature, while seeking opportunities to optimize processes and offerings.

1. What steps will be taken to encourage employees to adopt an attitude of continuous improvement?
2. Which initiatives will you initiate to foster innovation and experimentation in the organization? 3. Long-Term Growth Strategies

Develop a long-term growth strategy in line with your company's vision and goals, and identify expansion or diversification opportunities.
1 How will you implement a growth strategy to ensure sustainability and competitiveness for the business?
2. What measures will be taken to diversify revenue sources and expand into new markets?

**Strengthen Resilience:** Strengthen your business's resilience to manage future challenges by creating risk management protocols and contingency plans to handle unexpected circumstances.

1. How will you identify and mitigate risks that could threaten the business's stability?
2. Which strategies can be implemented so the organization can quickly bounce back from future setbacks?

**Engaging Stakeholders**
Retain the trust and support of stakeholders by regularly informing them of your company's progress and successes to instill confidence in its future prospects.

1. What strategies will be employed to keep stakeholders updated and engaged throughout the transformation?
2. Which approaches will you utilize to maintain positive relations with all of your stakeholders while showing commitment to their interests?

**Measuring Success and Key Performance Indicators Data**

Establish Key Performance Indicators (KPIs) to track your business's success and progress towards long-term goals, and regularly analyze performance data to make data-driven decisions.

1. How will you identify and track KPIs relevant to the business's long-term success?
2. Which measures will you put into place to ensure ongoing tracking and evaluation of performance metrics?

Celebrate the successes achieved during a turnaround and sustain momentum for growth and resilience, positioning your business for continued success in an ever-evolving business landscape. Remember, transformation is ongoing - with proper strategies and mindset, your business could even thrive more than before! Congratulations on successfully completing "Revive and Thrive: The Art of Business Turnaround!"

# Chapter 12.A

## Thriving in the Future: Maintaining Resilience and Exploring Unknowns

Over the past chapters, we uncovered key components for a successful business turnaround, from visionary leadership and crafting a rescue plan, through collaboration, continuous improvement and adaptability, to resilience building and accepting the unknown - as business landscapes constantly shift and organizations must remain adaptable and forward thinking to ensure future success. As we reach the final phase of this transformation journey, we focus on maintaining resilience while welcoming change - for success to occur over time.

### Maintaining Resilience Amid Uncertainty

Sustaining resilience requires organizations to anticipate potential challenges and disruptions despite uncertainty, and create plans to navigate turbulent waters successfully.

Walmart Inc. is an excellent example of a resilient business. During the COVID-19 pandemic, Walmart quickly adjusted to meet surging customer and employee demand for essential items as quickly as possible while protecting customer and employee health. By rapidly scaling up e-commerce capabilities and offering contactless delivery options quickly during pandemic times, the company flourished during an otherwise turbulent situation and cemented its place as a retail leader (Source: "How Walmart Beat Amazon in the Pandemic" by Matthew Boyle and Ben Steverman of Bloomberg).

**Investment in Innovation and Emerging Technologies**

Success in the future requires organizations to commit themselves to innovation and invest in emerging technologies. Staying abreast of industry trends requires staying at the cutting-edge with emerging tech solutions in order to gain a competitive edge and remain at the top of industry expectations.

Tesla Inc. is an excellent example of investing in innovation and emerging technologies. A pioneer in the electric vehicle market, Tesla continually pushes the boundaries of automotive innovation through their focus on electric vehicles, autonomous driving technology and renewable energy solutions - revolutionizing automotive industry standards while positioning Tesla as a leader of sustainable transport (source: Tesla Official Website).

**Cultivating an Agile and Learning-Oriented Culture**

Organizations looking to embrace the unknown should create an agile and learning-centric culture within their organization. Employees should be encouraged to experiment, learn from errors, and adjust quickly as situations evolve.

Airbnb Inc. is an excellent example of an organization successfully cultivating an agile and learning-centric culture. From its inception, Airbnb experimented with various strategies to reach its target market and then iterated on both their business model and design based on user feedback -

ultimately playing an instrumental role in disrupting the hospitality industry (source: Leigh Gallagher's "The Airbnb Story: How Three Ordinary Guys Disrupted an Industry, Made Billions...and Created Plenty of Controversy").

Fostering strategic partnerships and collaboration is integral to success in today's ever-evolving environment. Organizations can utilize external partners' strengths to gain access to new markets, technologies, and resources.
Apple Inc. is an example of how strategic partnerships and collaborations can foster business growth and user experience (source: "The Innovators: How a Group of Hackers, Geniuses and Geeks Created the Digital Revolution" by Walter Isaacson). Apple collaborates with chip manufacturers and app developers in order to enhance its products and ecosystem, contributing to Apple's continued growth while offering users seamless user experiences (source: Walter Isaacson's "The Innovators: How a Group of Hackers, Geniuses and Geeks Created the Digital Revolution").

**Implementing Sustainable and Social Responsibility Practices**

Thriving in the future requires adopting sustainability and social responsibility initiatives. Companies who prioritize these areas earn customer and stakeholder loyalty and trust.

Patagonia Inc. is an excellent example of a company embracing environmental and social responsibility through innovation, using recycled materials in its products, advocating for environmental issues and building customer loyalty (Source: "Let My People Go Surfing: The Education of a Reluctant Businessman by Yvon Chouinard).

# Conclusion:
## Take Advantage of Transformative Journey

As we conclude our journey together through the dynamic world of business turnaround, I invite you to reflect upon all that we've learned together: from visionary leadership and collaboration to embracing adaptability and planning for the future, we have unlocked secrets to achieving sustainable success amidst uncertainty.

On these pages, we have witnessed the incredible power of human ingenuity and resilience. Visionary leaders guided their organizations toward greatness with unfaltering determination; collaboration yielded exceptional results; individuals united as one formidable force created innovation that transformed industries and touched lives.

Continuous improvement has long been our compass, leading us toward an environment that welcomes change with open arms. We have seen how companies flourish when their cultures foster a growth mindset while encouraging employees to innovate fearlessly and accepting failure as an opportunity for future success.

As we contemplate the vast expanse of the unknown, we realize we stand on a precipice of infinite opportunities. The future presents itself with challenges and untapped potential that await us; with knowledge of innovation and emerging technologies at hand, we stand prepared to create something incredible.

But our journey doesn't stop here; now lies in your hands to take action and embark on your transformative path. As a visionary leader, aspiring entrepreneur, or dedicated team member you have the power to inspire change within your organization and shape its destiny.
As such, I encourage you to approach business turnaround with compassion, empathy, and an unwavering dedication to making a positive impactful. Foster a culture of continuous improvement where everyone's voices and ideas are heard and valued; dare to adapt with agility while anticipating the unexpected; embrace sustainability and social responsibility

because our collective actions shape our collective futures.

With Microsoft, Apple, Tesla and other industry leaders' lessons etched deep in your heart, you are equipped to embrace the unknown with courage and resilience. Every challenge represents an opportunity; each setback provides the chance to move forward more strongly than before.
As we bid you farewell, know that your transformative journey has just begun. The business world awaits your visionary ideas and unyielding determination; together, let's shape a future where innovation, compassion, and sustainable growth reign supreme.

Do not be scared to transform, for the possibilities are limitless when embraced with an open heart and determined spirit. Your story has yet to be written - make it one of triumph, resilience, and greatness as we enter this dynamic world together and create a better future together!